AMAZON FBA: SELLING GROCERIES AS A PROFITABLE NICHE

Plus 20 Grocery Categories You Can Start Selling In Now to Make a Steady Income!

Contents

Introduction

Imagine life without Amazon; impossible, right? That's how important Amazon is in our lives. Selling on this online marketplace is one of the hottest business opportunities of the 21st century. Looking around online you can spot countless entrepreneurs who sell products on Amazon: household items, books, electronics and so on. Amazon is an amazing marketplace where you can avail the unique opportunity to sell groceries to people looking for them. This is truly like discovering a very profitable and lucrative niche in the market. Were you even aware of the fact that Amazon sells groceries? Ever wonder how you can up your game the same way?

If you are looking for a way to take advantage of this lucrative niche in the market, you have to know how to go about it. A good idea with a bad execution is nothing but a waste of time, efforts and resources. If you are looking for strategic ways to succeed, then you have definitely come to the right place. This guide has been dedicated to exploring the best ways to sell gourmet and grocery items on Amazon. In this guide we will explore the many facets of this business- from becoming a trusted seller, to choosing the best possible items that will get you the most revenue.

It is important for readers to understand that even though they may already be doing everything to make it big on the website, getting orders and making a profit out of your Amazon business requires more than an online presence and a bag full of grocery items. Hence, thinking of this as a complete business is the best way to ensure that you put your heart and mind into ensuring you sell what customers want to buy.

This guide will highlight some of the rules, regulations and policy changes that Amazon enforces, enabling you to choose the right products in light of these restrictions, and then market them in the best possible manner. If you are unfamiliar with the many selling techniques that can be adopted when selling on Amazon, the contents of this guide will be a great resource for you to benefit from.

Ready to make notes? Here goes!

Why Choose Amazon for Selling Grocery Products?

A mazon has become a household name. Being an American e-commerce company, Amazon started as an online book retailer in 1994 and slowly started to sell far more than just books. Be it CDs, clothes, jewelry, electronics, grocery or household items- just about anything under the sun is available on Amazon. From a garage, Amazon expanded into the multi-million dollar online platform it is today, the largest internet-based retailer in the United States.

With dedicated retail portals in many countries apart from the U.S., Amazon's presence in the global marketplace is now hard to ignore. No matter what your business idea is, it can be implemented via Amazon and its wide base of customers all around the world. The service portfolio of the company is very diverse.

Apart from simply acting as a trading platform, Amazon also provides cloud computing services, offers music and video streaming, and has a number of other smaller websites under its flagship brand. Goodreads, Brilliance Audio and Audible.com are some popular names on the list of companies that are part of Amazon.

Unlike other online retailers, the population of buyers and sellers on Amazon increases on a minute-to-minute basis. As of 2012, the gross revenue of the website totaled a whopping $61 billion and currently the website has 209 million users. These users belong to different countries, which means that the trading portal is up and running every minute of every hour, around the clock.

At the end of the day, Jeff Bezos is an entrepreneur and Amazon is his brainchild, which is the same combination that many other small, start-up companies have. However, what is different about Amazon is its continuous efforts to innovate, develop and serve its customers better than before. In 2012, Amazon spent $4.6 billion towards market research alone.

Because of such intensive market research, one of the most useful services offered by the company is Fulfillment by Amazon.

Fulfillment by Amazon - The Star Service on Amazon.Com

If you already sell on Amazon, you are probably aware of its many features. But have you ever used these features and services? Do you even know what they are? Many times, sellers are unaware of the various trade features that Amazon offers on its web portal because they feel they are either too complicated or just not designed for them.

However, the thousands of sellers on Amazon.com who are successful at selling and making a profit- all thanks to the new and upcoming features of the website- are testimony that using these facilities and features is highly beneficial. It is because of the innovative services offered by Amazon that traders are able to make money from the comfort of their homes.

Fulfillment by Amazon (FBA) is one of the top reasons why people use this online marketplace to conduct business and trade. It is a dedicated service for sellers that takes warehousing responsibilities off their shoulders and makes it a part of the services offered by Amazon itself.

If you sell grocery and gourmet items on Amazon, chances are you are using the FBA service provided by the company. Via this method of selling, you leave storing, packaging, shipping and inventory keeping of the items to Amazon, while all you do is label and send the required items to the company's warehouses, and promote them online.

FBA has made it extremely easy for sellers to sell perishable items on Amazon by subtracting the logistics from the equation. Not only does this result in a lot of time-saving, FBA has amazing results on productivity and efficiency. By having little to no responsibility for storing and looking after the products you want to sell, you can focus your attention on promoting them instead.

Moreover, FBA has led online sellers to higher profit margins. Costs tied to inventory management and the storage of grocery products are significantly reduced and instances of timely delivery of perishable goods increase. According to a survey, 71% of Amazon users who opted for FBA experienced a sales growth of 20% as compared to when they first registered online.

The FBA does, however, charge you a storage fee whenever you send your products in to Amazon. The website categorizes its sellers into two categories: the individual and the professional. As such, fees will vary with each account so it's wise to pick the one that best suits your needs.

The success stories of using FBA, especially for grocery products, are many. While an online business on Amazon gives people the time and resources to follow their passions without being tied down by a 9 to 5 job, FBA takes this prospect further by streamlining the entire logistics and supply chain network for selling delicate and perishable products.

Therefore, by using the services and trading features provided by Amazon, you can start selling and making a profit easily. Still, keep in mind that one feature alone is never the key to success. While FBA is a promise by the company, what are your goals as a trader on Amazon? Which grocery product are you selling? How strategic is your approach to attracting buyers, and is the grocery/gourmet item really what they want to buy?

To improve your grocery selling business, it is necessary to have this 'mix' in perfect balance. You may choose a grocery product that is easy for you to access, but it may not be popular with the target audience. Alternatively, you may be selling an edible product that no one is aware of. It is these concerns that need to be answered before you can expect to generate healthy revenue.

A Quick Rundown of Rules You Should be Familiar With

Amazon's Rules and Regulations

Selling grocery and gourmet products on Amazon is very different from selling CDs, magazines or novelty china. You will be amazed to find out that grocery items make up a huge product section in the Amazon online marketplace. There are many sellers who deal with grocery and gourmet products on a daily basis, making it one of the hottest business ideas on the website.

In fact, online grocery selling has been called the 'next big thing', with the Amazon market and FBA services leading this sector of the trading industry. Currently, there are close to 200,000 different grocery items being sold on Amazon. Hence, if you are wondering whether groceries are the right product to sell, clear all doubt from your mind.

Before you set out to make improvements to your business, it is important to look at the many rules and regulations Amazon has put in place with regard to selling groceries and gourmet products via the portal. Since these items are perishable and can only be used within a certain timeframe, Amazon has developed a separate set of rules to govern grocery warehousing and delivering.

Additionally, Amazon limits the addition of new sellers in the Grocery & Gourmet Food category to ensure that customers are able to buy with confidence from all sellers on Amazon. The grocery category now requires approval before you are allowed to sell and the requirements can be found in Amazon's seller help section. The requirements for selling in the Grocery & Gourmet Food category reflect customer concerns about product quality, product branding, and consumer safety.

As a seller, you should make sure that you follow these rules strictly, because failure to do so will lead to unnecessary delays in shipments and, consequently, unhappy customers. Make note: the first and foremost thing to keep in mind to make your Amazon grocery business successful is to sell in accordance with the given rules.

Here are examples of Amazon's requirements concerning grocery and gourmet products:

- Have the following clearly mentioned on the packaging:

  - Product name

  - Expiration date

  - Name and address of the company that has packaged the product

  - Net weight and quantity, excluding packaging

  - Be properly prepared, checked and sealed to avoid leakage or breakage during shipping, handling and storage. The liability of shipping the product to Amazon via the best and most appropriate means lies on the seller's shoulders.

- Have a shelf life of greater than 90 days.

- Be removed from inventory when the expiration date is within 50 days.

- Be discarded, and not returned, in case the seller has opted for FBA.

Besides these regulations, there is a list of products that the company has prohibited from its forum. Examples have included the following:

- Infant formulas and foods that are not registered or licensed.

- HIPP milk products and formulas sold in the market.

- Formulas for infants that contain goat milk.

- Certain products from Sincerely Nuts like:

  - Yankeetraders Brand Crystallized Ginger Slices

  - Sincerely Nuts Ginger Slices Crystallized

  - Dried Crystallized Ginger - Sincerely Nuts

Moreover, for beverages, examples of the following specifications should be kept in mind:

- Custom Variety Packs for beverages like coffee should be sold in unit count sizes only, in multiples of 10, i.e. 10, 20, 30, etc.

- If one pack contains two or more varieties of beverages, both need to be in equal proportion.

- The packaging must detail information such as brand, type and flavor.

- A custom brand name such as your own company's name cannot be included on the packaging. Instead, the pack should simply read 'Custom Variety Pack'.

It should be understood that these rules, regulations and policies are subject to change any time, without prior notice. The examples provided above are meant to give you an idea of what some of Amazon's past requirements have been. Amazon often changes the rules that apply to grocery selling based on how well the sector is doing as a whole. Therefore, make sure that you keep checking these regulations to stay on the top of your game!

Prime Eligibility: Why is it Good From a Seller Standpoint?

Have you Considered Amazon Prime?

Amazon Prime is a membership program for those shopping on the website. It offers these customers a number of benefits that make purchasing easy and hassle free. Some of the most attractive prior benefits of being a Prime member have included:

- Free two day shipping on Prime Eligibility products

- No minimum purchase requirement

- Discounted one day shipping

- Free release date delivery for New Releases

- Prime Instant Video (unlimited streaming)

- Prime Members can invite up to 4 people living at the same address to avail these shipping benefits as well

- Prime 30-minute early access to deals

- Kindle early access to download books

These offers are attractive to a buyer looking for discounted deals and offers on Amazon. It is for this reason that purchasers take time out to explore and look through the website to get their hands on Prime offers that are budget friendly. However, these are the current benefits offered and are subject to change at any time.

Amazon Prime is predominantly for customers, i.e. buyers, not sellers. So why should you be concerned about it?

Why Should your Products be Prime Eligible?

Let's go back to your main objective for selling on Amazon. What are you after? Sizable revenue. Sellers who have been maintaining a business on Amazon for years have developed a great standing with their target audience because they offer exactly what the market wants.

These sellers have put time and effort into researching the kinds of services customers want and the way they want to be treated. Amazon Prime is a particular favorite among those who purchase groceries and other items from Amazon on a regular basis. While Prime Eligibility is automatically added only for products sold by Amazon itself, sellers can opt for providing buyers with these benefits as well.

Many customers who have signed up for Amazon Prime and paid the additional fee for it, often *only* do business with sellers who are willing to offer free two day shipping and do not have any minimum purchase requirements. Since they want to make use of the additional fee, these buyers are on the lookout for Prime Eligibility products to help them save some money.

Since the percentage of these customers is high on the website, and the percentage of third party sellers willing to offer Prime Eligibility is smaller, there is a big chance of attracting customers and making sales. Imagine if you make your grocery items eligible for free shipping via Amazon Prime and many of your competitors do not, don't you have a higher chance of securing sales?

From a seller's point of view, Amazon Prime and its benefits are very important because they mean:

- More business, by attracting some of the most active customers on Amazon who make grocery purchases in bulk.

- Since your product page will offer free two say shipping, for instance, the conversion rate on your online store will be high because customers usually try to save as many shipping dollars as they can.

- Amazon Prime results in customer loyalty and repeat purchases of grocery items, which is exactly what you need for your Amazon grocery business to become successful.

- With the stamp, 'Prime Eligibility' you set your Amazon website apart from others like it. Since there are thousands of people conducting the same business on the platform, setting yourself apart from them is the best way to stand out from the crowd.

We have previously discussed that an online e-commerce marketplace like Amazon is already cluttered with millions of buyers and sellers. One can rightly question the small probability of breaking out of this clutter and making it big in the Amazon grocery business. However, there is always a chance to offer something unique and catch the buyer's attention.

With all these benefits for a seller, it is highly advised for you to have your products registered for Prime Eligibility. This registration is available free of cost to all sellers. Moreover, while the major costs of FBA and Amazon Webstore still apply, Prime Eligible Products are given discounts for multi-channel fulfillment rates at the current time.

This is particularly beneficial if you sell grocery products that are unique and are not available in every locality of the city or country. Coupled with this specialty factor, Prime Eligibility can be used as a marketing tool to attract and retain buyers.

Groceries You Can Sell to Earn Substantial Revenue

You can have all your strategies in place, your future plans and objectives set out and your marketing tactics thought out, but if the product you are about to sell is not right, all the other efforts are futile in making your business successful. No matter how well planned and thought out your business moves are, the bottom line is that the grocery product you sell should be in demand in the market you target.

The importance of choosing the right product to sell can never be stressed enough. Even if you are a stay-at-home individual running a business on Amazon, a little product research is necessary. Many small-scale traders overlook the research phase because they either underestimate the competitiveness of Amazon or overestimate their ability to sell.

Either way, having the wrong grocery products- even with the right strategies- will only hasten the demise of your start-up. As mentioned previously, Amazon has a total of 209 million users and 2 million sellers. These numbers are *huge.* Imagine this many people physically buying and selling in a marketplace in your neighborhood. How hard is it for one seller to attract a sizable amount of the market share?

This situation is characteristic of the online marketplace. There are millions of people, selling millions of products, all of which are quite similar in nature. Hence, it is hard for one seller to stand out from the others and claim that his or her product is the best of all. The least you can do as a seller is to identify a product that is sure to sell and then market it well.

Apart from the cluttered situation of online trading, those buying grocery products online have a number of options in front of them. They can either purchase the same items from a physical store, like a neighborhood Walmart, or they can order the products from other sellers on Amazon.

With loyalty ranking low and the cost of switching suppliers being zero, customers are more powerful today than ever before. If they do not find a product, they will simply look for another supplier. This is one of the biggest reasons why grocery sellers on Amazon often bundle up a number of products and sell them together- a concept that will be discussed later in the book.

If you want to improve the way you sell gourmet items on Amazon, you have to understand the nature of these products and the way customers purchase them. Since grocery products are bought on a continuous and ongoing basis, you should choose items that are most frequently needed.

Moreover, since you are sure that a customer will always need coffee in his home (unlike a coffee mug, which is a one-time purchase), choosing the right product essentially means that you are making sure that the customer visits your online store repeatedly. This is perhaps the biggest benefit of picking the right grocery products right from the start.

Last, but definitely not the least, profit margins on regular, everyday kitchen and refrigerator products are already quite slim. This means that while you may earn a profit, it will not be significant if you only sell a few products from your portfolio. Choosing the right combination (i.e., most wanted) of grocery products is the best way to make sure that customers purchase sizable amounts, thus giving you sizable profits.

The same also determines whether your business attracts a regular stream of buyers. While it is necessary to attract new ones every now and then, customers that always purchase from you matter the most. Sustaining this crowd with the products they want is the key to making sure that your business is sustainable on Amazon.

For these reasons, it is crucial for you to put some time and effort into understanding which grocery products to sell, which ones reap the most profit and which ones should be there for additional and occasional sales. Always remember, the scope to make healthy revenue from online groceries is large, albeit difficult to cash-in for all the reasons discussed above.

How to Pick the Right Grocery Category

Now that you understand that choosing the right product can make or break your Amazon career, you will be willing to put the much needed time and thought into this process. Remember, there is no shortage of grocery products- not on Amazon and not in physical stores. Hence, those coming to you for their grocery needs will do so if they spot something that they cannot find anywhere else.

This means that your next assignment, after grasping the importance of picking the right product category, is to choose the product itself. Can you sell any type of cereal or sauce, or do you need to carry out further research on these categories? There is no straightforward answer to these questions. One look at Amazon's grocery selling business and you will see traders selling just about everything under the sun.

Easy availability of all grocery items and products has led to the development of a border-less online grocery market that directly competes with the physical market. The biggest advantage of the former over the latter is convenience, 24-hour access and no costs associated with driving to a grocery store, waiting in lines, loading the car, driving back and finally, filling up the pantry.

Putting yourself in the customer's shoes will give you a better perspective on this approach. For instance, if you purchase your regular groceries from a nearby store and you find everything you need there, will you be willing to change your supplier? The answer would most likely be no. When all your needs are met, why should you go through the trouble of exploring and finding a new store instead?

If, on the other hand, you fail to find some items in the store you visit often, you will be willing to look for other options. In this case, you may even be ready to pay a premium to have these items in your grocery basket every month. This is exactly the logic behind the Amazon grocery selling business you will run.

In addition, customers in rural areas that make use of Amazon Prime greatly benefit from it, since even a single grocery store is far from their reach. The stores are not cost effective to visit regularly, so shopping with a Prime membership, for more common items may prove to be a viable solution in the long run.

In the previous section, we discussed that Amazon displays a list of products that are the most sold online. These grocery items are in demand either because:

- They are cheaper than those available in stores.

- They are a better, healthier alternative.

- They are available in bulk.

When picking grocery items you should keep these characteristics in mind. Always try to pick products that move away from the regular options. Instead of selling regular ketchup, sell one with reduced sugar. Instead of selling regular orange juice, sell the variant that has cholesterol-lowering power.

Do not be mistaken; these products are not mystical or imaginary. They are available for purchase in many physical stores. However, they may not be sold by a local grocery store in your area, which is exactly what you will capitalize on. Buyers who do not want to go across town to buy ketchup with fewer calories will simply purchase it in bulk from your online grocery store.

Another great way to decide what to sell is to consider the bundling option on Amazon. Bundling refers to selling multiple products that are related to one another. For instance, if a buyer looks for marshmallows on Amazon, on the same page he will be told that the product can be bought with a certain brand of cooking chocolate as a combo deal.

The price of this deal is usually lower as compared to purchasing both separately. These 'bundling' deals make sense, but they also have a psychological effect. Even if a buyer does not need the cooking chocolate with the marshmallows, he will be willing to take advantage of the combo and save a couple of bucks in the process. Such buying behavior has become common and is therefore a great way for grocery sellers to decide on the list of products they should be selling. If you go with the same marshmallow and chocolate example above, here are a few ideas on how you can bring a creative twist to your grocery business.

Color-themed Varieties: You will notice that many sellers on Amazon sell colored varieties of the same marshmallows that you will find at a nearby neighborhood store. However, when available in different colors, these become attractive edibles that fetch a high price. For themed parties and events, these colored marshmallows are a big hit. And not just marshmallows; vendors on Amazon now sell color-themed candies, chocolates and other edible items.

Holiday Varieties: Want to have Christmas delicacies all year round? During the holiday season, special marshmallow filled candies with holiday jingles on them are a particular favorite among children and adults alike. Making these available even after the holiday season is a perk you can offer your customers on Amazon. Selling Christmas-colored marshmallows in different shapes and sizes is one way to customize to your grocery list.

Health-Conscious Varieties: Health consciousness has become a popular trend. Even when people want candies and chocolates, they look for varieties that have a minimum number of calories. Selling dark chocolate with a high percentage of cocoa is one way to put a healthy spin on your marshmallow bundle. Since these varieties are not always available at every local store, you can update your grocery business to cash in on this trend.

Tips for Choosing Grocery Products

The following are some essential tips to help you pick the right product and product categories to sell on Amazon:

- Choose a product that has a USP (Unique Selling Point). For instance, the low carb, low fat alternatives to edible products are quickly gaining popularity in the world, with an ever-growing demand amongst weight watchers.

- Choose a product that is not easily available in a particular area. For instance, if you live in a suburban locality that doesn't have access to products like dietary supplements and fitness drinks, you can start your business by identifying this niche.

- Choose a product category to sell instead of just one product. For instance, if you choose baking goods, sell a range of high-quality products in this category to encourage bulk and bundled purchases.

Food Categories That Will Maximize Profits

What Types of Groceries Sell Routinely on FBA?

One of the best sources for finding the right grocery products can begin by searching Amazon itself. Being a great online forum for selling, the website gives a detailed list of the most sold grocery products, which is updated hourly to give a realistic picture of grocery transactions. Going through this list is important for all those who want to start in this business sector or simply want innovative ideas about what to sell on Amazon.

Based on the number of sales of each grocery product, the list is endless! More than a hundred pages of grocery items only goes to show that as a seller in this category, you can do a lot to spike the sales figures in your store by simply choosing the right kind of products.

Since you are looking for ideas to sell food categories on Amazon, the following are some great grocery picks to include on your Amazon Store. Through trial and error, I have found the following 20 categories to be the most lucrative.

1. Aromatic Coffee:

Coffee is one of the staples on every grocery list. While a home never really runs out of regular coffee, the trend for aromatic and special-blend coffee mixes is on the rise. Many of these are freshly ground, mixed and sealed so that the aroma of the coffee is not lost even if it stays on the shelf for a long time. Selling such coffee blends is a great idea. Include coffee varieties that have special ingredients like chamomile, green tea or Brazilian coffee beans, all of which have beautiful aromas that are soothing and refreshing for the nerves. You can add these and many other kinds of aromatic coffees, so that buyers can choose the type and blend they prefer. Moreover, you can also add depth to your product lines by providing whole beans, ground, medium roast, dark roast, creamy, decaf and espresso. Since these are not available everywhere, customers looking for larger SKUs of aromatic and specially blended coffees can visit your Amazon grocery store to make their purchases.

2. Beans:

Beans are a delicious addition to breakfast, lunch and dinner. Hence, they are usually present in the pantry of every home. Apart from selling the basic red, white and green beans, as a seller on Amazon you can explore a number of different categories of beans. A particular variety called the Soup Mix has all these beans combined in a certain proportion. Altogether, red, white, brown and green beans are a delicious pick that can be added to soups to make them warm and creamy. Apart from this, you can also sell organic black beans, baked beans, mashed beans or re-fried beans, all of which are special varieties not available at smaller grocery stores.

3. Chocolate:

Chocolate is always high on Amazon's most-selling grocery items list. Many vendors sell chocolate on Amazon, either at reduced prices or bundled up with candies and other sweet-tooth picks that make for a great deal. If you want regular sales, make sure you include chocolate in the grocery list you prepare. There is a lot you can do with chocolate. One option is to sell variety packs, for instance, selling different flavors of M&Ms in one large pack, especially for parties and events. Similarly, such variety packs can be sold for all kinds and brands of chocolate.

The second option is to sell specialty versions like the Lindt Valentine's Collection. These are wrapped and presented beautifully and are always in demand. Assorted chocolate collections are another type that can be sold online because they are not easily available at local stores. Chocolates that are used as party favors usually have a theme. These are an attractive option on Amazon because people who arrange parties frequently rely on online vendors to deliver special varieties in bulk, like Robin's Egg Blue Hershey's Kisses.

Italian, Swiss and English chocolate is considered a delicacy in many countries. You can capitalize on this demand and sell specialty chocolate to a local market willing to pay premium for these varieties. Ever heard of spicy chocolate? Add the Tabasco Spicy Chocolate pack to your grocery store for health conscious buyers.

4. Whole Grain Products:

Whole grain products are very popular nowadays. People who are conscious about fitness and want healthy alternatives for rice, pasta and bread often opt for whole grain varieties. On your website you can include whole grain, raw options like roasted cereals, organic whole grain pancake mixes, organic whole wheat bread flour, wheat pastas (different shapes and sizes adds a lot of choice), whole grain figs and date snack bars and whole grain muffin mix. On the other hand, you can also sell prepared whole grain products. Some examples in this category that are top-sellers on Amazon are whole grain tomato and basil ready-to-eat pasta, multi-grain crackers, whole grain thin cakes, whole grain bread crumbs and whole grain with beans.

5. Dry Fruit:

Dry fruit is high in demand in cities that experience harsh winters. Hence, selling it on Amazon attracts a huge crowd because exotic varieties are not available all year around. The use of dry fruit in baking and cooking is another reason why it is always in demand. Dry fruit gift trays are sold by a number of sellers on Amazon. These trays are a collection of many different varieties of high quality dry fruit, and they make a perfect gift for a housewarming party. If you haven't seen dried banana slices and Goji berries at the local grocery store, you should definitely start selling these items online. Not only are they bought by many health conscious people, they are also popular as snacks for children. Individual 4-pound packs of dried cherries, berries, mangoes, pineapples, prunes and lychees are some types that are available at specific department stores. Selling those online means making these accessible to people right at their doorstep. You can also include organic dry fruit products, mixed dry fruit party packs and dry fruit and nuts souvenirs as well.

6. Mushrooms:

Dried and canned mushrooms come in many varieties. These can be sold on Amazon because mushrooms are a popular ingredient in Asian, Continental and authentic Chinese dishes. Local stores do not always have all types of mushrooms in stock except for the basic white ones that are available in cans. To include a lot of mushroom products in your grocery list, you can consider selling raw mushroom cans as well as prepared and semi-prepared foods. Bundling both products together in a deal will make a better combination and urge buyers to spend more time exploring your grocery range. Some ideas for the raw and value-added category are sliced mushrooms in a stir-fry blend, dried mushroom medley, mushroom spreads, cream of mushroom soup, mushroom popcorn, mushroom pasta sauce, dried oyster mushrooms, mushroom steak sauce, organic cream and mushroom soup, low sodium mushroom blend, coconut curry with chicken and mushroom, mushroom flavored soy sauce, whole button mushrooms and organic mushroom tea.

7. Dried Herbs:

Herbs are necessary in every household. Apart from the basic ones such as coriander or basil, exotic herbs like thyme, and oregano, used in small quantities, are essential ingredients in many cuisines. Using bottled herbs is also convenient for a home cook. However, they are not always available at small and local stores. Some options to include in your Amazon store are dried dried lemongrass, dried parsley and basil, freeze-dried red onions, salad seasoning herbs, mixed poultry herbs and dried peppermint leaves. Apart from this, organic varieties of the same herbs are also high in demand because they are fresher, free of chemicals and have a distinct aroma. Consider some popular organic picks like organic rosemary and organic ginger root.

8. Dried Spices

Spices are an essential commodity no matter what kind of a cuisine because they have universal appeal. For instance, red and green chilies are available in many stores but there are also more exotic options that people cannot find everywhere. Indian food is another form of cuisine that uses many different spices that may not be readily available in all parts of the world. Even within well-known spice categories, there are many variations (e.g., smoked paprika, hot Hungarian paprika, Spanish paprika, etc.) that buyers will be searching for to stock their pantries. You cannot always find these variations at grocery stores, particularly in certain areas, but they can easily be purchased on the Amazon Store.

9. Canned Vegetables and Fruits:

Besides dried fruit, canned fruits and vegetables are also an essential item on most grocery lists. They are easy to use and have a lot of flavor, which is why many people opt to buy canned fruits and vegetables in bulk. Varieties that are top sellers include sliced fruit cans (peaches, pineapples, papayas), canned fruit medley, canned green beans and chilies, canned and preserved mixed vegetables, canned and sliced carrots, and baby corn. The same canned fruits and vegetables are also available in organic form. To make it even more specific, you can sell canned fruits of a particular type. For instance, canned mandarin oranges are not available at all grocery stores. Buying them online is cheaper and much more convenient for orange lovers.

10 Beverages:

One look at Amazon and you will realize that half the grocery sellers stock a huge variety of beverages. Since beverages can be purchased in bulk (bigger SKUs) and stored for weeks on end, they are a safe and easy pick. Moreover, there are many options within this product category that are imported from other countries or made with special requirements. Hence, a beverages section in your grocery store is necessary. Apart from selling the most popular colas and sparkling water, another option is to sell variety packs of fizzy, carbonated drinks; for example, packs of sparkling juices, vitamin water, energy drinks and iced teas. These packs include different flavors, which makes them a popular pick. Another line of beverages you can stock up on is flavored milk. Since these are a favorite amongst kids, they are purchased by parents on a regular basis. Introduce flavors that one cannot find easily at a local store. Cold coffee tins, fruit juices and herbal teas are some options that will help you attract coffee lovers, fitness fanatics and teens as well.

11 Snacks:

Snack items are easily available on Amazon in bulk. Large boxes with 40+units of various snacks are purchased by customers to stock up their pantries at very reasonable rates. Some of the most popular snack items include chips, cookies, granola bars, fruit snacks, nuts, crackers and sandwich fillers. Multi-flavor packs of chips, rice crackers, cheddar crackers, cereal bars, dried fruit snacks, peeled mango bites, and trail mix party packs are some of the most popular picks on Amazon. To take a look at how well the snack category is doing, go to Amazon and simply scan through the endless pages of snacks that can be sold in bulk.

12. Baby Food:

Baby food is a specific product category that is targeted at new mothers. Again, like all other grocery items, baby food is bought in bulk. However, since most parents prefer to add different flavors and nutrients to their child's diet, they buy different varieties that include vegetables, fruits, nuts, protein and a lot of good fats. Many times, local stores do not have all such varieties, which is why people buy baby food in bulk from Amazon. Options within this category include organic baby food, baby food paste pouches, baby food oatmeal, baby food crackers, multi-grain baby cereals, baby food that has vegetables with chicken, and variety packs with a combination of these.

13 Vegetarian Items:

If you want to target the vegetarian section of a grocery store, there is a lot you can sell on Amazon. From raw vegetables, canned and preserved mixes, to ready-to-eat vegetarian foods, all varieties are popular amongst customers looking for specialty veggie delights. In fact, there are many vegetarian products on Amazon that you have never seen on the shelves of local grocery stores. This means that selling vegetarian diet items, such as vegetable protein chunks, organic mushrooms, vegetarian beans and vegan pork shreds, is definitely a great way to increase your online sales. In ready-to-eat vegetarian foods you will find miso soup, no chicken noodle soup, veggie hamburger mix, vegetarian sausage mix, fishless tuna, and vegetarian chili and beans.

14 Baking Goods:

In baking items, raw ingredients as well as prepared mixes top the grocery list. Some popular products are specialty sprinkles, flavorful cake mixes, decorative icing, colored fondant, innovative shapes in cake and muffin pans, gluten-free bread mix (which would only be available at special fitness stores) and flavored chocolate chips. These baking items are used in novelty cakes and cupcakes that are made to order. Hence, their availability is usually limited to expensive stores only.

15 Wines:

Amazon Groceries is nothing less than a specialty winery. The most common SKU is the three-pack variety combo that comes in a multitude of flavors. From regular wines costing 20 to 30 dollars, to specialty wines costing more than 100 dollars, all options can easily be sold on Amazon. Holiday gift-packs of high-quality wines are also a big hit on Amazon. Apart from this, other products that contain wine include wine crackers, wine gums and wine mixture pouches.

16 Non-dairy or Gluten-free Items:

The most popular ready-to-use non-dairy products on Amazon are coffee creamers, macaroni and cheese meals, Greek yogurt, dark chocolate chips, etc. These items also come in different flavors. People who are looking for healthier options such as gluten-free brownie mix, raspberry cookie mix, red velvet pancake mix, mini fruit and nut energy bars and various whole grain products can find them stocked and available on the Amazon store.

17 International Recipes:

International recipes belonging to Mediterranean, Chinese, Japanese, Continental, Indian and Arabian cuisines are an instant sell on Amazon. These recipes are either available in powder or paste form, and are part of a large variety of flavors, spices and herb categories that have a separate, specialized section in homemade foods. In very few grocery stores does one find packs of ready-to-cook Indian delicacies. Examples of such items are seasoning mix, packs of Indian curry mix, ready-to-eat spinach with oil, chickpea curry, tuna salad snack, potato dumplings, pasta and vegetables, and many more. Hence, selling these items on Amazon means filling a separate niche altogether.

18 Special Food Items:

There is nothing like the amazing holiday foods one gets to enjoy during festive seasons. Specialty cookies, candies, sour treats and the many more amazing options that are usually labeled 'limited edition' all fall under this category. Since these are always in high demand, as a seller you can take advantage of this market. Gift sets and variety packs are the highest selling SKU in this category. Therefore, selling assorted holiday cookies and candies during the off-season is a great way to make an extra profit by charging premium prices.

19 Pet Food

If you have a pet then you most definitely know what a struggle it can sometimes be to shop for their food. However, that problem can easily be solved by opting for the Amazon store where you can find plenty of pet food, including dog food, cat food, small animal food, bird food and fish food. The pet food is available in a variety of sizes and flavors. You also know that the food stored at Amazon is safe and healthy for your pet.

20 Gourmet Food

It is truly rare to find good gourmet food items anywhere, which is why Amazon takes the credit for introducing great quality and cost effective gourmet food options for people who are looking for them. They have a large variety of gourmet foods that people can choose from according to their own personal taste in food and cooking. Amazon offers varieties of beverages, breakfast foods, coffee, tea, snacks, stews, soups, curry sauces, pastas, and more. You can also find gourmet gift packs for spices, snacks, candy, cheese, coffee, fruit, seafood, tea and jams within the Amazon store.

Tips for New Sellers

Since it is an open marketplace, hundreds of new entrants set up their websites on Amazon with detailed product listings and descriptions every day. There is always room for more sellers who bring in a variety of grocery products, fueling competition and hence stabilizing prices. Since Amazon has turned into a highly competitive e-commerce forum, it is integral for those who are setting up stores to learn the tricks of the trade and equip themselves to sell efficiently.

Getting help from those who have been selling grocery items on Amazon for a while now is a great way of getting hands-on knowledge about this business. As mentioned previously, taking a structured approach towards becoming an Amazon grocery seller is essential before you can expect profits to roll in.

However, it isn't uncommon to see sellers on Amazon opening trading businesses without a formalized or structured approach. For them, running such a business is a whim or impulse, and this usually results in failure. Though Amazon has introduced a number of services and facilities like the FBA, which make grocery selling easy and hassle free, a strategic approach must be adopted nonetheless.

Keeping these points in mind, the following are some tips for new sellers who want to make it big on Amazon:

- Do not treat your Amazon Grocery business as a 'side thing.' Accept that you do not have to leave the comfort of your home to run this business, but this does not mean you should take it lightly. Being serious and having a 'give it all' approach is the most important prerequisite.

- Plan, plan and plan some more. Adequate planning is essential to selling groceries on the website. Many sellers who sell Christmas candies on Amazon all year long have put in a lot of thought and planning to make sure that customers are attracted and 'hooked' to their grocery items all year round.

- Avoid getting in trouble with the administration. The expiration policies and rules laid down by Amazon should be followed at all times. Having your products listed off, dumped or simply under notice by the administration can hurt the credibility of the business badly.

- When picking products to sell, always try to cash in on some extra feature or specialty. For instance, if you sell a product that is only available in your region, you will be able to leverage your sales instead of having a non-specific appeal.

- Don't be afraid to add variety. Many grocery sellers simply overlook the prospect of deepening and widening their product lines. Over time, when you have created a customer base, adding new products will help retain these customers and attract new ones as well.

- When customers receive grocery products that are crushed, leaking or just improperly packed, they are put off and discouraged from placing an order again. Since hygiene is a big factor when it comes to perishables, a seller should pay particular attention to packaging.

- Do your homework before joining the grocery selling business. By this we mean that before you set up your Amazon store page, spend some time researching where you will buy the products, what rates will be offered, what price you will sell them at, and finally, the profit you will reap.

- Opt for the FBA service. Reducing the amount of work you

have to do, even if it is at a higher cost, is a great way to focus your attention on customer service and the timely processing of orders.

- When adding product images, be mindful to upload an image that is a true reflection of the product you will sell. Avoid tricking the customer with flashy and unrepresentative images, because clear pictures make the decision-making process faster and hassle free.

Conclusion

The marketplace for grocery selling on Amazon is still in its infancy; however, thousands of sellers have started selling and an equally strong number of buyers have switched to Amazon for their daily and monthly grocery needs. Run a search query for Amazon's grocery business, and you will find hundreds of results online.

The topics discussed above are a brief guide to help you improve your selling propositions on the website. This guide is by no means an exhaustive discussion, because mastering the art of selling groceries on Amazon will require ongoing education and innovation. The more groceries you sell, the better you will likely become at generating revenue.

While the various grocery product ideas given in the book are the perfect starting point for new sellers, they also alert existing sellers about gauging the effectiveness of the kind and type of grocery products they are selling on Amazon. Hence, when deciding on your product, spend some time researching the local and online market to identify niches that you can exploit. Products that are unique or have a limited and seasonal supply are the best opportunities on Amazon's grocery list.

Lastly, you reap the benefits of the Prime Eligibility feature the website offers. Amazon Prime Eligibility is very important from the seller's point of view as well. If Prime customers regularly purchase their grocery items from you, it is a sign of credibility and exceptional quality. Benefits like these make it necessary for grocery sellers to constantly look for better and bigger opportunities in order to serve their online market.

Got a second?

Thank you for purchasing and reading my book! I hoped you liked it and was able to gather some valuable information.

Can I ask a quick favor?

If you liked this book, I would really appreciate if you could take a minute to leave a review on Amazon. I love getting feedback from my readers and read all of my reviews!

Sincerely,

Eric Hall